RISE AND FALL:THE UNPREDICTABLE LIFE.

THE JOURNEY IS BEAUTIFUL THAN THE DESTINATION.

ANCHAL SINGH

ISBN 979-888569194-9

This book is dedicated to young and old, literate and illetrate,employed and unemployed,each and every person to remind you that you are precious,you're loved and you deserve everything in your life.Stay true to yourself.Work hard, and never give up on your dreams, even when nobody else believes they can come true but you. These are not cliches but real tools you need no matter what you do in life to stay focused on your path.

In the history of the universe, there has been nobody like you and to the infinity of time to come, there will be no one like you. Existence should have supported you so much that it broke the mould after making you, so that another of your kind will never get repeated. You are original. You are rare. You are unique. You are a wonder. You are a masterpiece.

Today is hard, tomorrow will be worse but day after tomorrow there will be sunshine. Don't be afraid of death, be afraid of an unpredictable life.

Contents

Foreword

Life is yours.You're the one who will define the meaning of life and it is valid for you only. Everyone lives with different reasons to accomplish different purposes ,keep searching if you didn't find yours.Think upon this what you want to achieve in your life journey - life with dreams satisfied or life with treasure of money with no satisfaction. Make this human life a meaningful era.

My reason to live this life is to enjoy the small things that life brings with it. The small surprises that age brings with it.I want to experience everything that comes along my way. Though a few things might turn out to be painful one's but at the end of the day there will be one thing that will bring a smile on my face. And that smile of mine is one thing that I want to treasure.

Smile is the most honest thing that any person can possess. It doesn't lie. It infact manier times brings a smile on others' face too.So, maybe there are many difficulties in life, there are a few moments that you would never want to miss. Look around you, you can change this world, you can give someone a hope, you can give someone a chance, you can give someone your smile, there so much to do if you live and that's why you should live.

Thus we are living in a hope that we could die at peace.Do everything that you had ever wished in your life. And for sure you have to do a lot of hard work in your life to gain that life. Do everything that could lead to your target by only thinking about it.

It is true that you came with nothing in the world and would also go without gaining anything but you can earn happiness of others and can spend it by gaining happiness.

Make yourself that everyone could say at your death that you had lived your life before anything else.

Preface

I know right now, you all are struggling. It feels like life is going on without you, like there's some party, everyone is happy around you and you don't know how to react.

Maybe you failed in something and everyone is against you. But eventually, the clouds will clear. Eventually, the sun you thought was permanently lost will shine again. Maybe not today. Maybe not tomorrow. Maybe not as quickly as you'd like but you will be okay.Don't underestimate human strength. You are a resilient creature far more powerful than you realize.

The bad days don't stay bad forever.The struggle might lead to success; remember, one day, you will achieve greater heights. I know you're tired even though you just woke up but just do your best today. That's all anyone can ask of you. That's all you can ask of yourself.

Don't push yourself too much. I know you're scared to fail. So much so, you're striving for perfection and you beat yourself up every time you fall short. You're your own worst enemy and I'm here to tell you, you don't need to be.I know you're worrying and thinking too much.

I know you failed,but let me tell you one thing 'Andhere ko andhera nahi,sirf roshni mita sakti hai.' Good days are coming.

This hard time, this anxious time, this troubling time — it won't last forever. It's a harder phase of life. It's an exhausting time of life. But it will lift. You just have to keep going. You deserve happiness, and it will find you. It will just take time.

Life has seemed like more of a battle than a blessing lately, and every time you finally seem to be away from battles, life only seems to knock you back down. These are the days that can either destroy or define you, and it is up to you to decide which path you take. I hope you don't let it destroy you. I hope you get back up every time the world expects you to just give up and stay stationary. Today may not be your best day, and tomorrow might not be either, but I promise you that one day, you will wake up and realize this is the beginning of everything you have ever wanted.

Please don't give up on your dreams and the life will give you something unexpected. Ek din aapko kuch aisa milega,jiske baare me aapne sapne me bhi nahi socha hoga. It is up to you whether you want to move forward or stand still thinking about your failure; but know that if you choose to stay exactly where you are, you will never know how far you could have gone.

Don't let people convince you that life is better lived when you don't have any ambitions or dreams so you don't get disappointed. You can be happy, your time is coming, you just have to believe that you deserve it and the rest will follow.Say to yourself-This too shall pass.

Thanks for reading!

Acknowledgements

Writing a book wasn't easy at all.It was more difficult than I thought and more rewarding than I could have ever imagined.

First and foremost,praises and thanks to the God,the almighty for his showers of blessings through out the journey of writing this book and to complete the book successfully.

Nobody has been more important to me in the pursuit of this book than the members of my family. I would like to thank my parents, whose love and guidance are with me in whatever I pursue. They are the ultimate role models. Most importantly, I wish to thank my sister, who has always supported me in authoring this book and I really appreciate it.

Also,Having an idea and turning it into a book is as hard as it sounds.It wasn't possible to complete this book without the support of my teachers and friends.I would like to thank them for helping me in gathering lots of information from time to time in writing this book.

I want to thank everyone who ever said anything positive to me or taught me something. I heard it all, and it meant something.Thank you,thank you so much!

This life may end the next second and I may not leave anything to this world except some beautiful memories to some and some really bad ones to others. I will try to add some knowledge into the lives of those who cannot afford it.I would give a smile to the world. And I'm sure that I will get it back always because smiling for someone is sweet;but making someone smile is the best thing.

Last but not the least,To whoever is reading this;I want to say that stay optimistic and always look for a positive sign out there. Please, I want you all to never ever give up in whatever hard work that you are doing my readers.May God bless you all.Always stay happy and always stay positive! You're precious,you all are amazing!

CHAPTER ONE

~ Little Journey: A life full of challenges. ~

Life is not what is given; it is how life is taken. Attitude makes a lot of difference in one's ability to feel happy. A man who cannot buy sugar for milk will be glad if he happens to come across one who cannot afford to buy salt for rice porridge. Look at the poor people who cannot get a square meal a day. Such comparisons will help in boldly facing the challenges. The inner strength, faith in one's capabilities, will power will enable one to face the challenges. One may not succeed in one's attempt but achievement includes failures also. Remember the first time heart transplant was done. It was a success because the patient survived for fourteen days; at the same time the patient's death was a failure. Still,it was a great achievement in field of medicine. So,optimism makes any problem a challenge.

If you look a challenge as a problem probably it's your negativity but if you look a problem as a challenge; it shows your positivity and a strong will power.What i meant is that; keep setting goals. Either wanted or unwanted,have courage to sort them out because we are never meant to just give up.

Accept the challenges that comes in your way.Life is very short. Incredibly short, so try to make the most out of it.Grab the opportunity,do not look east or west,Just give in your best.

Sometimes, there is no room for failure. Sometimes, perfection is the only option. Those are the days when you feel most alive, most useful, because you know you can succeed, though it may only seem with ease to those around you who don't understand what you're doing.

God has sent each of us into this world to spread happiness, and peace; but today we all are so depleted that we have lost the image and quality of ourselves.We are a pure, peaceful being, peace is our nature. To bind every one with peace and faith we are here.To again recollect those dignity of ourselves with his power we are here,to rise, to fall,to learn, to experience, god has sent us.We all are angel's; it's just we have forgotten this thing.

Never compare one's life with other's. However,happy the other person may seem, its only that person who knows what struggle he has been doing to live in this competitive world. The grass always seems greener on the other side, so never follow any path just because it lures you.Instead, follow what suits you best and be satisfied with what you achieve.

There are many people in this world who dream of living a life that you live. People struggle to get food twice a day and we people complain for not having a specific dish. Do dream, dream big but also be contended with whatever you have rather than complaining for things that you don't own.

So,Lets reconnect with the one self, and know the purpose why god has sent us to this world. World is beautiful because god has created our world.

You have something in you which no one in the world has.Recognise it and work on it.It doesn't matter if you fail.If you keep up with it, someday you are bound to be successful.Every person in this universe is unique. If you succeed easily, you're simply not challenging yourself.

All the abilities are hidden in us, but they can be tapped only if we believe in ourselves. So, this time believe in yourself and do the right thing that is within your reach. This is a beautiful world. You are meant to face the difficulties and emerge victorious. All the difficulties are supposed to be tests in our life to test our strengths.

See,in our life there are people, who quit their life in between, because of very tiny problems. But, if we give a little more efforts, most of them would be resolved. Remember, No problem in life is bigger to quit the life itself. They just come & go and test our patience levels & how strong enough we are to face them.

When we pass a test, we are elevated to higher levels in life.We find new reasons to live. This life is precious. We should not waste it. It is only cowardly to do so.We cannot solve all the problems in our life ourselves. We need to find and take the assistance of right people.We are not alone in this world and we should live in a society; we should not be alone and till a stage.

Life is a process of discovery; it is a mystery; discover it and solve it! Also you need to get better in your behavior day by day and earn the good wishes of all around you. Then you have led a worthy life.When you have confidence in yourself, you know that you will do what it takes to get the goal completed.

No matter the situation you find yourself in, always remember that you are the most powerful person. No one else has the power to influence your self-confidence and self-esteem like you can,that is 100% on you.

You are the judge, jury and executioner of your own awesomeness,every single day.The more we get out of the way and stop worrying about how we are feeling and simply get on with whatever it is we want to do, the less any of it matters.Some days its sunny and warm and other days its rainy and cold,just like sometimes you feel confident and creative, while other times you feel insecure and stuck.Confidence isn't the problem.Your thinking about it is.

At times, you would need to shut the inner critic down. You would need to help yourself calm down by talking to yourself. At such times, you would need your own support, and you must be there for yourself. To support yourself. To talk yourself out from your anxiety and fear.At that challenging phase,no one will be there for you to support you.You have to be strong.

What if you failed?Try out one more time, you have nothing to lose, you can only succeed. Certainly giving up is not an option. Everyone has a talent and so do you. Let it shine out, is all you have to do.

Don't ask that how to manage time. Don't ask that how to utilize time. Ask yourself, how do I manage myself? Because it is the self that is wasting the time. It is the self that is wasting everything that is around it. The world in which we live in today, everyone is fighting a battle with time. Seldom do we finish things within deadlines.

Everyone is always running late when it comes to delivering the work assigned to them.We always think :How wonderful life would be if only I had a couple of more hours to finish this task. If you want to manage your time, you should focus on remaining busy as much as possible. The key is to not to get disheartened upon not achieving a small target in a limited span. If you can continue doing those small things, you'll wonder how in this world you could achieve the amount of targets which you otherwise couldn't in one month time!

Always remember one thing that your life does not belong to you only, there are so many out there who will be affected if something wrong happens to you. Like,truth is we cannot control every accident on the road but we can reduce number of accidents by following traffic rules. So most important thing is to keep yourself alive and healthy then only other achievements and success comes into the picture.

See, Perfectionism is a terrible thing. There is a fine line between wanting to do a good job and taking things seriously, on one hand, and being afraid to make a mistake on the other. Any time you do an unfamiliar thing, you are going to make mistakes. Don't be disturbed by this. With practice, you will get better. Focus on trying to get better, not on trying to be perfect.

Be your own best friend. Give yourself a break. Accept that things will not always go your way and that you will not always be the best you can be. Forgive yourself when you mess up and just focus on trying not to make the same mistake again.

Time slips from our hand like grains of sand never to return back - even the whole world's gold can't buy it dear.We get 86400 seconds everyday and we deliberately waste it. This time will never comeback. Life improves when you decide to do things differently. In this case, the goal is to gain control over time, rather than letting it control you. It is about taking ownership of time,which is the essence of your life.

The main objective of time management is for you to have a clear picture of your upcoming days, weeks, and months. It is a way for you to discover what time you have available to devote to study, recreation, or other activities. Make the decision to be the master of your life, rather than its suffering slave!

All these years we ask god for a number of things, but I want to be a person, god is proud of. Like he's given me every possible thing now it's my time to be the best human and return a good self to god.

• First of all, be a better person. Because if you are not a better person then no one will like you. So first of all have a better reputation in the society you live in.

• But in the race of being a better person do not forget who and what you are or what you want to be.

• Be what you want to be first, because the rest of the things can wait.

• Achieve something great. Different people have different thoughts about great things, so achieve something you think is great.

• Never stop trying. Life will give you too many failures, but never loose hope and always keep trying because someday you will definitely be successful.

Our present is the only thing you have in control, regretting about the past and worrying about the future is not going to solve any problem for you.If you want to be a better person, you need to stop dwelling on the past and worrying about the future. It's easy to go along with what everyone else is doing because humans instinctively want to be part of a herd.

Fighting that, in a way, is fighting human nature.But it just takes a little bit of observation to realize that the crowd is not always a good place to be.Being different from the crowd leads to bigger and better things.ff you want to improve your life in any way, observe what everyone else is doing and do the opposite.We are all gifted with energy to find a success in our life, but fail to gather a courage which is required to reach heights of success and end up clinging to the things that are familiar to us.We need to free ourselves from our comfort zone to explore new opportunities and find a success beyond our capacity.

Create a positive atmosphere - Positivity, happiness, excitement and joy are all things you can have and create as long as you practice them. You get more done when you are happy, are less likely to feel attacked when happy and are kinder, nicer and overall a better person.

Own up to your mistakes - Everyone makes them and a lot of people made worse mistakes than you have. Own up to your own mistakes and solve the problems you created. This is your life, meaning it is your responsibility, for better or for worse. Listen to the people around you - It's not about you. Every person has their own life to live and is the main character of another story! Sit down and watch their story unfold.Become interested in them instead of boasting about yourself.

Realize that no one is better or worse than you - Every human being on this planet is better than you and worse than you at some things. But the overall value of each individual is the same throughout. Once you can look down at the homeless people, the drug addicts and the people you hate and see that they are just as valuable as you are your whole outlook of the world will change.

Always act first - Don't wait for your friends to plan events and invite them to the things you planned instead. Stop hoping that person will message you, call you, or come and speak to you and go up to them yourself. And quit waiting for your life to magically get better and start to do the things ,you want to do.

Do it for others - You can live your life for yourself, but then you only have to cheat one person to distract yourself, relax or not do the work. But when you commit to a greater cause, to other people or simply to something more than just yourself then whenever you do not do it it is cheating the world. Do more things for others and you will actually do them, feel better about them and be more motivated every day.

Stop taking yourself and your life so seriously - This is not a life or death situation. If you think that way about life you will never enjoy any part of it. Stop taking every problem so super serious and just laugh about your own situation. It makes life so much more enjoyable when you learn to laugh about everything that happens to you, for better or for worse!If you want to be a better person then you're already being a better person. Today is the first day of the rest of your life. Get out there and live it.

Hope I, you and everyone else on this planet achieves whatever he wants.You've to think out of the crowd and to be a risk taker and challenging in your life.Life is beautiful when looked with a optimistic vision.

So, go ahead, and start off with a new life. Wishing you all the best in your learning journey! May you go on to produce something that you feel proud of and happy about!

CHAPTER TWO

~ Unfulfilled Desires: Taunts of the society. ~

We all have hopes and dreams. We all go through times in our lives when we come up with ideas of things that we would like to accomplish in life, places we would like to be in the years ahead.We all want to do something memorable.Afterall, It's a natural human tendency, it seems, to come up with an ideal that we would like to fulfill in our future time.If we have a dream and we are really passionate towards it,then nothing can stop us.We will always find a way to overcome the hurdles in our way.

Not everything in life can be cakewalk.We will have to run an extra mile to outshine and achieve our dream,our goal,our purpose of the life.

But what happens when the years go by and those dreams never turn to reality? What happens when we find ourselves, years later, in a situation that's so far removed from our ideal that we can only think that we've somehow failed, that we haven't accomplished our life's desire?

Let your heart guide you--if it tells you to stay, that's where you're supposed to be, and make the most of it. If it tells you to go, then take the risk and make the most of that. If faith in God is part of your life, ask him for guidance, then listen for the answer; and whatever that answer may be, follow it, for you will be taken care of.

The reason behind not converting our dreams and reality is the 'fear of failure'.What if we failed?What will people say then? See,there is no end to the expectations people have from you. The moment you go wrong, they start pointing at our mistakes. All the good done in the past is forgotten. Any small mistake committed then gets magnified. This is the nature of this material world.Don't listen to people's advice.

Life is yours.You're the one who will define the meaning of life and it is valid for you only.

Everyone lives with different reasons to accomplish different purposes ,keep searching if you didn't find yours.Think upon this what you want to achieve in your life journey - life with dreams satisfied or life with treasure of money with no satisfaction. Make this human life a meaningful era.

Million of people are discovering their highest and best potential, and understanding their uniqueness. You must have some kind of uniqueness some quality that makes you stand out from all the rest but some of us fail to recognize what we have been searching its already is inside us and all you have to do is align with it that's all it takes. Its part of you helps you to keep track with your life purpose and in touch with your passion and joy.Accept who you are even when others don't.

Take control of your self confidence, do what you want to do and do what makes you happy.Sometimes people don't like you or try to change you for being a real. Don't give yourself away at any cost. Trust me it takes of courage to be best version of yourself. You are the one who have the power to control how you are vibrating, positive or negative, what you think you become. What you feel you attract. What you imagine you create. If you don't like what you created, simply choose to change your thoughts to create a new reality for yourself. You are more powerful than you know.

Success is something which gives us unlimited satisfaction and happiness for the rest of our life. Success is different for different people.For some people success may mean money,wealth or possessions etc. But for me success is achieving true satisfaction and happiness.That's true,only few people get success in life. The reason is they dream big but are not willing to take any action towards achieving success.They often get distracted by temporary pleasures and thus lose the eternal happiness.

If you don't work for what you want in life then later on don't complain or give any excuses when you are working for someone whom you don't want to work for.

It is your own fault why you didn't achieve what you dreamt of long ago! When you see the brightest smile and happiness in your parents's face just because of you, yes it is great success. If you can reach a certain position in your life someday, from where you can look back at your experiences, and not regret anything about the choices you made, because they are the ones that got you there, then you are successful. Success is when your own opponents start praising and respecting you. It is when you achieve your goal that you desire. We all know that life is full of challenges and opportunities, but success comes to those who actually struggle to grab the opportunities and overcome the challenges.

Life is unfair for everyone at some point of our life,you look for something and something happens,slowly you look at your age and you think "Why doesn't it always happen the way, i want it to be,even though i have done my best?",That's because- you have no control over others and your dream job or dream girl or just anything.Its not about the time you are facing now,from birth till your death you suffer in many ways,everyone suffers.

Finally,what i want to say is hat whatever time gives you make it special,think positive and don't waste time thinking about problems,live your life,may it sound selfish in various angles but its fine. It's your life,you are not here to make everyone happy,you should be responsible for your happiness and no one else.Unexpected things happens always,lots of surprises are yet to come!

Even in unexpected situations and unexpected times,try becoming happy and think that we live only once. This life and this moment is not going to come again.

And yes "unexpected things happening at unexpected times are inevitable but suffering is always optional". Slowly you start loving yourself and one day may be you succeed in this that you realise you need nothing to be happy,and unexpected things happening at unexpected times is just normal.

Don't follow other's dream; instead follow your goals and dreams. You are not someone else; you have your identity and capacity and work accordingly in order to achieve the real success.Don't get disheartened, if you fail initially, instead keep trying. Remember that your mistakes give you valuable lessons in the end and also help you choose the right path.

Focus on what you want rather than what you don't. Be accountable for your actions. Everything and everybody has been designed with a proportion of uniqueness to serve a purpose that we can fulfill only by being our unique self. There was a time in this world when a Krishna was required and he was sent; A time when a Christ was required and he was sent; a time when a Mahatma was required and he was sent; There came a time when you were required on this planet and hence you were sent.

Let us be the best we can be. To think like a genius, you must see things in a way different than everyone else.I'd say in reality, everyone is capable of being a genius. What separates the genius from everyone else, however, is that he or she is able to see patterns in things that that most people will not see.

Maybe there are many difficulties in life,but there are also few moments that you would never want to miss.Look around you, you can change this world, you can give someone a hope, you can give someone a chance, you can give someone your smile, there so much to do if you live and that's why you should live.Thus we are living in a hope that we could die at peace.Do everything that you had ever wished in your life.

And for sure you have to do a lot of hard work in your life to gain that life. Do everything that could lead to your target by only thinking about it. It is true that you came with nothing in the world and would also go without gaining anything but you can earn happiness of others and can spend it by gaining happiness. Make yourself that everyone could say at your death that you had lived your life before anything else.

You can be as smart as you want to be, but the geniuses of the world are not recognized for their intellect alone: It is what they do with it that makes them excel in life and show how intelligent they really are. At the end of the day genius is determined by your persistence to your work and by going the extra 100 miles that no one is willing to go.

No matter the situation you find yourself in, always remember that you are the most powerful person. No one else has the power to influence your self-confidence and self-esteem like you can,that is 100% on you. You are the judge, jury and executioner of your own awesomeness,every single day.

The more we get out of the way and stop worrying about how we are feeling and simply get on with whatever it is we want to do, the less any of it matters.Some days its sunny and warm and other days its rainy and cold, just like sometimes you feel confident and creative, while other times you feel insecure and stuck.Confidence isn't the problem.Your thinking about it is.

If you go crazy for your dream to be true. It's all about your own hardwork,consistency and the firm self believe system on yourself. If you want your dream it's your own choice and all the way it's in your own hand.Work for it , give your best,and just be positive; keep no doubt on your capability, you'll definitely get your dream true.

The more efforts you put towards your goals, the better would be the end-results.The distance between dreams and reality is called action.Thinking about something isn't enough, you do need to work hard for it. Next, you need to believe that what you dreamt of will come true.

Also,some times we get confused about life because people interfere and put obstacles or pull us to other wrong/confusing paths, how ever, they are also humans and probably are really confused and don't know what they are doing, don't let other people confuse you.

See,If success was easy then many would be successful till now;but that's not true. The Problem is that everybody wants the prize but nobody wants to pay or willing to pay the price. Nobody's willing to make the sacrifice. Why are we talking about hard v/s easy?

Nothing is easy, So we should be like, we don't want passion easy. If it was easy, then everybody would be doing it. Right? If it wasn't difficult then everybody would be doing it. Everybody would be Successful in their career. Everybody would be an entrepreneur. Everybody would be a billionaire. Everybody would be a successful athlete, or artist, or businessman, or scientist, or salesperson. Everybody would be doing it,

Right? It not supposed to be easy. You shouldn't want it to be easy. But if you have a dream, if you have a mission, if you have a passion, all this is not going to be easy. Easy shouldn't even be in the conversation or in your vocabulary. This is supposed to be hard. You should want it to be hard because then no one can replicate what you create. Anything of value and of meaning's not going to be easy and that's how it is supposed to be. In short, Stop searching easy ways, try difficult too.

Success is guaranteed.Don't take always easy paths. It's life, not a dream because no matter how beautiful your dreams and fantasies are, you will always have to wake up and face the reality of life. Just know, when you truly want success,you'll never give up on it. No matter how bad the situation may get.

We have to struggle, struggle hard to get the name and fame. The struggle we are in today builds the strength we need for tomorrow. And these struggles make us rise high. It is not all about success that we get in life. Failures teaches us more to overcome and fight the struggles.

They give more strength to fight. Its true that success hugs and cheers everyone in private but failure punches everyone in public. Never ever get scared of struggles,just happily deal with them you will automatically achieve whatever you want in your life.

You never know what people are going through, they either maybe smiling and dancing with everyone but still fighting those demons every night.

Even the most intellectual people feel demotivated at times.The difference that needs to be noted is that people who are good at something would have been doing it even when they didn't feel like doing it.The key to stay motivated is to determine the purpose. Even when you are demotivated, if you recall the purpose of doing it, that must motivate you. For example: If you are studying only for the sake of marks, then please don't study. You can think life as a school which gives you knowledge in every single second of a life but terms and conditions are applied;and what terms and conditions are applied are given below.These terms and conditions are for all the people who study and don't study.

1.Never mind if you're doing something wrong but if you accept your fault and try to solveit then your life is going in right way.

2.Never forget your aim, without aim life like a brainless species which only want or need food to survive their life.

3.I want to tell you that never forget your parents dream; if you want to do something good than every times you need blessings of your parents but accidentally you fail to crack or achieve your goal that doesn't mean your life end, life will give you too many opportunities.So,try to make something great aim and try too hard achieving it.

Life goes on at the end of the day, remember it. And there is no problem with the present,its the past and future which become the root of all problems. Think about that.Maybe that guy you see going for a walk with his pet every morning,Or even the famous person, always cracking jokes, Or the best student of your class, teacher's favourite,Or even your mother, working daily going through so much everyday,Or your father, working so hard for you.These all people, you will never know if they are dancing in the rain, or carrying the half of the world behind that genuine fake smile.

You never know when they'll be so tired that they will just give up on their lives.And you'll stand there cursing yourself that why didn't you noticed earlier, but it will be too late.

You only get one chance to follow your dreams. Why would you follow one that isn't the best dream for you? Why would you follow just the first dream that came into your head, even though that dream might be all wrong and terrible for you.

Examine what you want in life, and why you want it, and make sure you can actualize that dream. Make sure that dream will fulfill you and enrich your life with joy and happiness and success and growth.

Make sure your dream helps others and gives you satisfaction in the helping. Make sure your dream doesn't harm others, or doesn't require you to ignore the needs of others.

You are a valuable and wonderful person who definitely has a spot to fill in this world. It doesn't matter what anyone else thinks. There is never a hopeless situation in life which can't be overcome. Change your lookout of life and try finding happiness in small thing.

It's okay to work for what you want. But, that doesn't mean that work is the only life. There is much more beyond that. Family, Friends, Fun, etc. Happiness doubles when you share it.Family, Friends, Fun, etc. Happiness doubles when you share it.

If you failed, although you tried, you must not let yourself down by sitting aside as life will not stop giving opportunities.Stay there,try and try until you achieve your target.Also, don't compare your life with others.

There are the people who give time for everyone who are important in their life & as a result, they live a balanced life. Not all difficulties can be solved alone. Sometimes, family & friends come to rescue. Everyone will be happy with their own life and others too. Happiness, Sadness, Difficulties, Fun, Emotions, Entertainment & many more.Life seems to be complete!

God gives all of us the resources equally!Everyone's life is unique & different!Our life depends on how good the efforts that we keep to design its best! We lose our value, when we compare our lives with others! You only have one life. Give your best & make it more colourful and meaningful.Destination is same, but what makes it more beautiful is journey of experiences, you go through!

Life is very precious. Don't think of giving up just because you missed some opportunities. You are one of a kind, enjoy your uniqueness and keep going. I feel, nothing is going to happen by just reading motivational quotes or reading motivational books. It is worth only if you apply it in your life.

Destiny is one thing that will shape your life but then there is two things that is known as determination and will power. If you are determined for anything or has a will power to change anything, then even destiny will become your fan.

Some people are given more opportunities and facilities in life, but that is not necessary that they might understand the game of life well enough to play it intelligently and win. While there are people who are not born with a silver spoon in mouth but with their intelligence, power and an understanding of the game of life they change the way things were to happen. Seek Not to find Who you are, but to determine who you want to be. Stop looking for a purpose as to why you are here, Create it.

Just one decision and you could change your life forever but its up to you weather you want to act or not. If you want to change your destiny, you can. For that,you have to fix your goal. You need to make a step wise ,time bound programme. It may be to be day -wise, week - wise, month -wise, then year -wise, as per requirement. A close follow up is required.

Glass is always filled and never empty.Even when you don't see anything in it, it's filled with air. Look for happiness which you are not able to see and I am sure you will bloom with smile. If your dreams do not come true at all, then remember you may have something in your destiny that you may not have dreamt of and which is definitely better than your dream.

Lastly,be patient. At times, things take longer than expected. Good things come to you when you least expect them and when the time is perfect for them to happen. So, dream until your dream comes true.

CHAPTER THREE

~ Difficult Road: A Beautiful Destination. ~

When something bad happens, we tend to blame god and ask why god allowed this to happen.When ourlimited and narrow minds begin to analyze god, we often fail and we get emotional.For any bad situation, things will either get better, stay the same, or get worse.

God tests you first. He will put you in a situation to test your efforts. He will definitely help you once you are through with the test. You just have to give your best in anything that you do and always remember that he is there with you.

The world is happened inside you. The outside has triggered it, of course but it's how you feel and what emotion gets triggered is completely in your control. You just need self mastery. Once you achieve that, there's no one who can stop you from getting whatever you want in the material world or other dimensions.

We just need to believe that god help us with our life problems but you need to also understand that we
cannot understand how god does that for the reasons just

stated. Sometimes you only see god's fingerprints inyour life but when you look back;you realize that where you are now is a result of the design by the divine.

See,everyone in this world will pass through tough situations but many people me away from it.They don't know that at once they have to pass through it anyway it may be tomorrow or a week later or even a year later.

Be positive,think that good time is on way ;you just need to reach there.Think,that this time will make you more stronger and you would acheive more in life.You get these times in your life to put you to test and get the best out of you.

If you succeed to overcome your difficulties you become a winner. However, if you don't succeed even after having given your best, you atleast can say you gave your all.

But, if you didn't try and gave up; you might regret later of letting an opportunity go away. Because often such hard times are blessings in disguise, but only if you are able to see it that way. There is just one thing that makes your dream impossible,the fear of failure.So,you don't have to fear.

Everybody will advise you, what suits them more.

- When you will start doing something new, people will advise you not to do that. Because no one has done this before you, so you can't do as well.
- If you are strong enough and continue your mission, they will start telling you, how to do it correctly.
- If you will continue doing your stuff by your own way, they will start laughing at you and make fun of you.
- If you still didn't give up, many of them will become your enemies and create hurdles for you.
- And then,in the end, you will win the game but they will again start coming to you, saying that they always

believed in you.

So, train your mind to see difficulties or hard times as opportunities to bring the best in you and not as something to discourage you or put you down. Another point is, to be with encouraging people around you and avoid people with a negative mind set.

Firstly accept everything that has happened, or rather happening. Do not try to change the things which you can't, as in that case they will end up taking your control. We always wish positive things to happen in our life. But if everything happens in the way we have planned, then we can never learn anything new. And for learning something new, we need to pass through challenges. So the first thing you need to do is to accept all the negatives, however hard it might be.

When we lack a stable sense of self, we might not know what we feel. To be able to deal with emotions, we need to understand them first and we need to understand who we are as a person. It is important to recreate genuine connection with ourselves, to be able to operate in this world effectively. Having a weak sense of self (and the resulting sense of emptiness) is often caused by being raised in a toxic family, in which we were likely taught that "it's not okay to be me." We should relearn how to love ourselves and care for our inner child, and to fully accept our identity.

Answer these questions: who are you, who do you want to be and what are the steps to achieve that. Every time you take one of these little steps to give yourself credit for it, praise yourself. You need to be the first person who loves you most.

Start small and keep pushing yourself, keep experimenting and keep going. What you're experiencing has a purpose.

Now what you need to do is to change your perception about life. Change your mindset regarding all the negatives. Don't try to control something that's out of your control. Instead think what you need to do now from which you'll be benefited. Keep yourself busy in things you like.Make self-improvement your prime goal. If you want change, then be the change.

Try your best to ignore all the negatives, and focus on your goals to become a better person. Work on your weaknesses and make yourself strong. Remember, challenges come in our lives in the form of negatives, and it's our responsibility to fight through the odds and emerge victorious. After all you own this life of yours, why are you wasting it on the negatives?Won't you regret for it later?

Decisions play an important role in our life. Making a right decision is really tough. We don't know if our decision is going to prove beneficial in the long run. Yet, we have to make a decision. Once we make a choice, we cannot go back, as one decision leads to another. To restart life from a convenient point is not easy in life. We can't go back and correct ourselves, as we have travelled a long distance. What we can do is that we have to be very wise and careful, while making a decision. We have to visualise the possible consequences of our decisions and then make the best decision as far as possible.

Both people coexist-the one who push you up and the one who pull you down. But you always have a choice. Choose wisely.

When you get into a tight place and everything goes against you,till it seems you could not hang on a minute longer; never give up then,for that is just the place and time for you that the tide will turn.For life is a either a daring adventure or nothing.

You don't have to blame anyone, you just decide to remain positive and work towards overcoming your problem and things will start moving in the right direction.

I wish I could tell you that things are going to get better soon, and that things will never be awful for you again. But I won't lie to you; life will be more unfair and harder for you than for most. While life may be worse for other people, it is still all right to be upset with your circumstances.

There are some things people shouldn't have to live with. Even if you can survive something it doesn't mean you should have to, but you can, and you will. Things are going to stay hard for a while, and I am so sorry it will take so long for you to start getting the good things. But I promise the good things are coming, you just have to survive.
Say it until you believe it: everything will be all right.

When you are surrounded by negative people throwing negative ideas at you all the time are also working for your advancement in a way - They are telling you what is not to be done in a particular instance thus helping you eliminate some of the possibilities that you may have thought of. So take it in the right spirit, lend a ear to them, keep the second to throw it out of your mind, all the time grinning from ear to ear and thanking them for their ideas. Go back and do what you think is the best possible solution to the problem and move on.

When negativity comes, accept it, and then move on. You don't have to stay there. You control your own attitude, and your attitude means everything. Instead of viewing situations and events as problems, view them as challenges.

Do not let these people go to your head. Because that would be a dangerous situation to be in. So the best way to tackle such people is to acknowledge their presence but dismiss their thoughts from your presence!

You know what? When you will start climbing a ladder, people will try their level best to pull you down but when you will reach the top, those same demons will say "We knew you will achieve something great in life."

You are the master of your life and destiny. You create your own life. You are here to learn lessons and do your life purpose.

You are a free soul, spirit, an energy pattern. Be the best person you can be. Be good, kind, sharing and understanding.

Everyday is like a blank book, and the pen is in your hands. It is your chance to write a beautiful story for yourself.My ultimate resolution is to stay happy,to believe in myself and work hard to achieve my goals,to make my parents proud through each and every way i ca to find positivity in every negativity,to try to bring smile on anyone's face atleast for once,to stay away from all that darkness in which i will never find light,to spread positivity to all the corners where my aims can be reached and to be a better person than what i was perviously.

Don't bother about what's happening all around. Even if the whole world around you is positive and only good things happen you can still harbor negative thoughts! The power to think and choosing our thoughts is in our control.

There is so much positivity also around. Try to look for it and you'll find it. You know something? You will find what you are looking for! So, start looking around for positive things and you'll find them.

Believe that whatever happens is for your own good. Believe that you might not like what happened right now — but that it'd serve you in the future.

Think for a second, every bad that has ever happened to you, don't you some good it brought to you after all these years? Sure, not all cases aren't like that. But most cases are!

Start believing. Start the journey to positive thinking. And your whole life will turn around within no time. You'll enjoy every experince regardless of its positivity or negativity. You will have a great zest for life.

CHAPTER FOUR

~ Be yourself: Make your weakness,your biggest strength.~

We care less about ourselves then others,we know less about ourselves then others ,we are less influenced by our own thoughts than other's comment. We see less of what we have acheived than what are missing. So,how can you motivate yourself with thoughts of others in mind ?

Trust me, you can read hundreds of stories of success and failure but none of them will motivate you long enough .All those external thoughts will be eventually discarded by you own thoughts; this is your life, and it's ending one moment at a time, the only thing you can do is play a bigger game by investing in yourself.

You are born into genius and life is too short to play small with your talents and today can be the first day of whole new life.Just remember one thing that no one is born with perfection you have to put your efforts to make things on your side.

Have a moment with yourself and just allow your inner self to speak up and follow your real dream, do not look somewhere else.

Much of life is about competition. If you don't know what you're capable or incapable of, you choose the wrong battle. It is very important to know your limits, and maybe how you affect other people weather good or bad and of course if that's bad try to change it. Its always important to know yourself so that you can always better yourself where needed.

Be confident in your intentions and keep your eyes ahead instead of wasting your time on those who want to drag you back. Because you can't change people's views, you have to believe that true change for yourself comes from within you, not from anyone else.

Remain simple! Do not try to become something. Just remain as you are. Simple, ordinary! Do not try to become something, then everything will be alright. You will feel light. You will get rid of a lot of burden.

See,If you want to get motivated every single day then you should watch some motivational videos which will give you energy to turn all the winds in your direction but this motivation is a temporary one and it reamainsoutside. It depends on us how we use time and turn the winds in our favour.

I know you want to get things easily. You want to achieve everything in life but as per your thinking, you need to watch motivational videos on youtube to get motivated. Do you believe that it is going to motivate you?

You know what, sometimes if whatever you have read or seen is really powerful and conveying it may give you a surge of adrenaline and you will eventually feel a little better full of energy. But that will not last for more than a few hours.

So, isnt there something in this world that will motivate you and others who feel a little demotivated or demoralised;there is.There is only one and only one entity in this world that will keep you motivated each and every second ofyour life.It will live with you and it will die with you and i have to say that it could the most sustainablesource of motivation a person could ever have.

If you haven't got it till now, let me tell you;It is you,it is you and your failures.It is your very little achievements.The only thing that can motivate you is you yourself! You will be there for yourself through every little upsand downs of your life.You can make a difference if you believe in what you do.

You can't change what already happened;but you can change what will happen. So, it is all about your perception and attitude.I would suggest you to stop getting yourself investing emotionally on anything you come across.

At the same time, do not stop enjoying the life.Enjoy your every moment and do not expect anything from anyone.

1. It is your life and you should control it and not influenced by other's decisions.

2. Now,it is time to focus on change and accept the changes. Listen to yourself, you know what is best for you. You would rather take a wrong decision than someone else taking it for you. Be responsible for yourself.

3.Don't give up after the first failure.

See,If you believe in something that you wish to achieve, if you know that you have the capacity to go out and face the storms, beat all the odds and get back on your feet every time you fall, then no matter what others say to you, you will succeed. People will come and doubt you, but if you are patient enough and keep your efforts in the right direction, fate will take its course. All good things to those who wait.

My whole point is that don't let petty issues bother you;your life is more important than all this.Rest you know the best. You are strong person and can do well. Believe in yourself!

When you start something and get stuck somewhere hardly you would look for some motivation on the internet.I would say,just look at yourself.Why did you started? Look into your past,learn from failure!
If you believe in yourself and what you do then I don't think you will be ever going to search for an answer to get motivation.

If you want to do something different in your life then you need to get inspired from within. You require a big cause for doing a work.Then you don't have to set alarm you will automatically wake up at 5 'o'clock.

It is not that if you get inspired you will not face difficulties but for that you will not need daily dose of motivation. To get inspired from within you need to find find a cause which will benefit others not just you.

I know while doing any work many problem comes rather than beating your head on the problem think for the solution. There are many people in different fields who are successful. The thing which make them
different from others is their way of thinking and attitude.

Listen,you don't have to fight with others.You have to fight with yourself,you have to compete with yourself and one day you will reach at a point where no one can even imagine to fight with you.

Just remember two things, first that the decision belongs to you, you are free to listen to yourself and second, this decision will change your life, now it's upon you to mould your life into heaven or hell. Never lose your confidence in your choice.

People will be there to make fun of you, to criticize you, but you must have faith in your choices. Don't care about what others say except your parents. Remember:Kuch toh log kahengey,logon ka kam hai kehna(People will always say something, its their work after all).

Whenever anybody else tell you that you can't do it, just asked him/her why and interestingly he/she has no genuine reason of telling you that you can't do it and he/she was awestruck after listening your great reply to his/her non -sense belief. Take difficulties as a part of life and try to learn something new from everyday's life problems.Just think about success and leave no space for failure thoughts.Just believe in yourself.You will definitely achieve your life goal if you are so passionate and desperate in achieving your that particular target.

No matter what happens, however ups and downs you face, whatever bad phase you had and painful things you are going through, even if everything is going opposite of what you have planned for.At the end, you should be happy and satisfied that is what it counts.

The secret of becoming a better person in life is very short and simple. Your present is the only thing you have in control, regretting about the past and worrying about the future is not going to solve any problem for you.If you want to be a better person, you need to stop dwelling on the past and worrying about the future. It's easy to go along with what everyone else is doing because humans instinctively want to be part of a herd.Fighting that, in a way, is fighting human nature.But it just takes a little bit of observation to realize that the crowd is not always a good place to be.Being different from the crowd leads to bigger and better things.ff you want to improve your life in any way, observe what everyone else is doing and do the opposite.We are all gifted with energy to find a success in our life, but fail to gather a courage which is required to reach heights of success and end up clinging to the things that are familiar to us.We need to free ourselves from our comfort zone to explore new opportunities and find a success beyond our capacity. Create a positive atmosphere - Positivity, happiness, excitement and joy are all things you can have and create as long as you practice them. You get more done when you are happy, are less likely to feel attacked when happy and are kinder, nicer and overall a better person. Own up to your mistakes - Everyone makes them and a lot of people made worse mistakes than you have. Own up to your own mistakes and solve the problems you created. This is your life, meaning it is your responsibility, for better or for worse. Listen to the people around you - It's not about you. Every person has their own life to live and is the main character of another story! Sit down and watch their story unfold. Become interested in them instead of

All the best,you know what? You're one of a kind.Enjoy your uniqueness and just keep going!

CHAPTER FIVE

~ Failure and Mistakes: A Lesson,not a loss. ~

Failure is the biggest hurdle that can ruin your life if you overload your thoughts with it.There is only one failure in life which can not be fixed and that's suicide.

Failing is a part of life. It's not that you lose something. It's that you didn't gain something.You must be wondering how to prepare yourself for the second chance even if you gave your 100%.This time you have to learn a lesson what failure has to teach you.Failure teaches that you lacked somewhere. It dosen't tell you that you cannot achieve it or you are not capable. It teaches you to put some extra efforts where you lacked,teaches you to be confident,teaches you to be patient and prepare you to face difficulties in life because we are humans and everything in life dosen't run smooth.

You failed it's fine.But now learn everything what you can learn from that failure.Even failing can teach you great lessons of life what success may be couldn't. Implement those learning from the failure you got in your life and definitely the platform is yours and no one can stop you from getting a success.This time you are prepared.Not just prepared you are are completely prepared.You are prepared not only for this attempt.You are prepared for your whole life.

When you fail at something, once you acknowledge that it is a failure, also try to realize that it was also a potential success, and you will never fail in that exact same way again. Time has moved on, you have experienced something new, you have changed a little as a result of it. Even if you face a similar scenario in the future, it well never be exactly the same. If you survived this failure, you will survive the next. It will still hurt, it will still sting, you will wish to high heavens you had succeeded, but you will survive it.

Failure is inevitable, but your response to failure is not. You have a choice. You choose how you will respond to it. You choose to grow from it. You choose to see the good (the unrealized potential success), and you look forward.

It takes time, it takes will power, it takes a decision to try to see the good, through your tears, your hurt and your pain; but the moment you do, you'll realize how much better a person you've become. You will want to cry, you will want to yell and scream, you'll want to punch sonething or someone, and curse everything. You may want to curl up into a ball, and stay a perpetual thing of misery, but don't. Keep moving. Get up, dust yourself off, look around, and look for the next thing to give you comfort, to make you feel good.

Our body is like a hardware and our mind is a software and life is a game. Yes we do mistakes , we encounter failures but who doesn't. While you are playing a video game, don't you fall back and replay again so that you get back to the same level.Failure tells you your mistakes and makes you a stronger contender.

It's just that a video game is a lot more easy than game of Life. But treat life like a game and see the change. All the things will become simpler. Everything has a price and so does every single failure but it's not that big to give our entire time.

Time is precious. Instead of feeling disappointed move on as you do for the game. Dont be stuck in emotions and plan for your future. Learn from your mistakes and promise yourself to not repeat them.Thats all you can do and you should do.

Life has a lot more to offer and the best part is that there are no fixed levels.

Somedays the results — for whatever reason — won't be there, no matter our efforts, which is why we can't get caught up in the story of the day.

You took your prospective client through every cycle in the sales process, but they didn't buy. You spent hours on a post that nobody read, despite you feeling great about it.

Somedays, we aren't going to have the best of us in us, and we just aren't going to be able to articulate the success that we had envisioned in our heads. These are tough days. Even harder to accept.

Nobody likes losing or not getting the results that we are after.

Yet, it happens — despite our best laid out plans, our best efforts, and our best actions. These days will happen more often than we are willing to realize or accept.

The lesson isn't to accept losing or failure. The lesson is in understanding that failure will come — even when we put in our best effort — and we will not win every day in the pursuit of our goals. When we are pursuing great things, this is a guarantee.

Whether your chasing success in entrepreneurship, writing, or athletics — somedays, the results we hope and desire for will not be there.

That's ok. We will be ok.

Just believe in yourself and say to yourself that this is not the end. I am going to stand and prove myself.Don't let the failure define you. You are not born to fail. You are born to live, survive and face all of thechallenges that comes in your life.

No one has a perfect life. Look at great personalities and scientists, they have failed many times but never gave up on their goals and dreams.Follow your passion and your goals. Afterall, you never know what life has planned for you.So,always be happy!

You are yet to face the biggest problems in life. Learn to deal with the problems. Thinking about your failure again and again will not change the outcome. The more you think the more you get depressed. So, leave the past behind and focus on your future.

The road to success is unpaved, non-linear & full of hurdles. Every time you stumble, these lessons will always help you get up & continue with greater vigour. And remember that no dream, no goal is bigger than a man's determination to achieve it. Try focusing on it. Let bygones be bygones. Don't be disheartened. It's all just a part of life.

A few years later when you'll look back at this. You'll feel proud you have overcome your failure and worked on yourself untill you succeeded. Do not worry. And don't feel like a loser.

Failure simply means lack of success and until and unless you don't believe in yourself and your actions, you won't succeed.Any successful person will honestly admit that failure happens.I think we all have a fair share in it.There is just one thing that makes your dream impossible,the fear of failure.

Try to learn more, fail more, fail harder, learn harder. Because if you won't allow yourself to fail, then you won't know, how hard it is to stand again and fight for your dreams?Just overcome this fear, have confidence in yourself and whatever you do, one day you'll surely succeed.

Don't be that hard on yourself. Skip the rat race you are trying to win. Do not do anything just because you want appreciation or acceptance of the world and society. To be one amongst crowd is not success. A failure does not define who you are or what you might achieve in your life. Go higher, achieve bigger.

Why are you being sad and depressed? You have so much to accomplish. You will be fine. Stay strong, you can make it through these difficult times.

No one is going to remember you because of anything at which you failed at, people remember you for the legacy you leave behind. In the end, it doesn't matter, who you really are, but, what you choose to be and what you become;that only matters.

It is far better to fail at your own original works than to copy someone else and succeed in it.Every person in this universe is unique. If you succeed easily, you're simply not challenging yourself.

Sometimes, there is no room for failure. Sometimes, perfection is the only option. Those are the days when you feel most alive, most useful, because you know you can succeed, though it may only seem with ease to those around you who don't understand what you're doing.

Feel your emotions. When you feel you have failed, you may be overcome with self-recrimination, disappointment, and despair. Holding in your painful feelings can have negative effects on your health, your relationships, and your future success. Notice each emotion as it comes to you.

Accept what happened. After the first shock of disappointment wears off, work on accepting what happened. It will be harder to move forward if you blame yourself or others, or pretend that what happened didn't matter or didn't really happen. Write down or reflect on everything that happened, what lead to it and what the consequences were. State only the facts, without blame, judgment, or justification.

Identify fears that are irrational or excessive-

Do you worry that failure calls your intelligence and capability into question? Do you imagine that you are the only one who has ever experienced this setback and that you are being judged? Are you worried that everyone will be disappointed or lose interest in you if you don't succeed?

Failure is something that happens, not something you are. Be careful not to blur the lines between making mistakes and being someone who only makes mistakes. Our actions may define us, but our failures do not. The actions you take to move past failure and reach success will define you in the end. Failure can leave an open wound and it's unwise to ignore it. Without acknowledging it, your wound will continue to hurt, take longer to heal, and possibly get infected.

Do we stop driving after not getting driver's license on first attempt? Of course not. Then why should we stop living for a certain failures! Life will always through pebbles at us. Its much more challenging and interesting that way. If life would have been a walk in the park, then each day would have been boring.

You are naive if you believe that every single agenda you partake in will turn out the way you want it too.

A flipped coin can land on two possible sides.
Pencils come with erasers at the top.

That, we are prone to failure and making mistakes is a universal truth and one of the most natural of human phenomenon's which we struggle to accept.

Stop struggling.

You've probably had a run of successes in your life. This makes dealing with failure all the more difficult.

But just think about it, has not that feeling of euphoria that came with success passed as well?

Nothing lasts. Not success. Not failure.

People talk. Yes. But, should you let that affect your life in any way?

Luckily, people also come with un-retentive memories , and it's only a matter of time till they forget about it or simply grow tired of babbling about it.

Also remember, you have your whole life to change the way people perceive you, if that really matters to you.

Take some time off to reflect on your failure. Tell yourself that, It's nothing to be ashamed of.

Figure out where you went wrong. Re-plan, re-strategize. Bounce-back. Man,you are not defined by your failures but your ability to bounce back from them.

Enjoy it, smile. Failure is no reason for you to be unhappy. It's no reason for you to punish yourself.

When the results aren't there, and we don't have the storyline we prefer and have chased — we must understand what comes next. Resilience. The ability to keep moving forward.

There are lessons to be learned with everything in life but you have to be receptive to them and open for growth. Mistakes are inevitable but you can judge the true character of someone by how they respond to misfortune.

You are here on earth to fulfill a mission and purpose. It may be to help other people, be a good mom/dad, run a successful business so you can give more back, etc. If you quite and accept failure, then you are missing out on your mission. Most people are so close to success but they give up on the one yard line.

Family which is first and foremost in my life. They love you and need you. If you are ever feeling sad, make sure you give more and do more for other people. It will make you feel better.

Failure is just a stepping stone. I always say to fail forward and fail forward fast. Life will be hard sometimes but it is only temporary.

Time on earth is limited so you have to make the most of it. You never know when your time is up so get up and show up to the world. They need you as well.

Quitting isn't an option in my mind. There is too much to see and too many people that need to hear your message and see your talents.

What do most people do when the story and results aren't what they desire? Many people quit, get down, and allow the next day or task to be affected by this, which leads to more failure, self-pity, and yet another story, with less than desirable results. It's a vicious cycle, which, if we aren't careful, will continue to repeat longer than we would like.

By finding the resilience within us, we avoid this trap. We don't want to get caught up in the endless circle of failed results, self-pity, and no growth.

You have experienced disappointment and are frustrated, because something did not turn out the way you expected, but you have not failed.

It's easy to get overwhelmed by the seemingly infinite problems in the world. It happens to all of us who care, and want to make a difference in the world.

Sometimes we've made a difference and we don't even know we've done it. A smile or a compliment to a stranger, a helping hand, a random act of kindness. These things matter. They matter a lot, actually.

There are people whose lives touch millions, and who make huge impacts, and become well known. But most of us are not those people, and that's ok. Do what you can.

And don't stop caring or trying. An opportunity may come your way, and that will be your chance to make a huge difference. You never know. You're here for a reason and you're not a failure.

Whenever you feel low or failing in something then stop thinking for a while and give yourself a break for sometime. That period makes you rock strong and teaches you many important lessons of life which helps you grow as a better person. But again it depends on person to person.

Patience is the key to success so during bad phase of life if you keep yourself calm and with all patience passes that difficult time with all positivity then no failure in life can make you feel sad and trust me success will come to you in all good ways soon.

You can only be assured of failure if you give up.

There are so many variables that go into making any effort successful, and most of them, particularly if other people are involved, are beyond your control. Why should you accept or admit failure for variables beyond your control? Why should you admit failure if you've learned what to avoid in the future?

One thing you can control is whether you are doing your best. If you are not doing your best, no one else can do it for you. It's okay to feel disappointed, even frustrated, but it is important to understand what you can and cannot control.

What happens usually is that our emotions get the better of us - for some people one or two failures will break them, some others 100 or 200 failures would still not be enough to stop them from moving forward. The latter group realizes that everything is still going as per plan and that failing was a part of the plan to begin with.

So you can say that difference between Elon Musk and 1000s of other researchers who tried to make a working fuel cell for automobiles - is that they may have stopped at 100 failures and Elon Musk just found enough determination to go fail several hundred more times until that one success.

Remember the story behind Edison's 10,000 attempts to create a light bulb or Dyson's 5,126 attempts to invent a bagless vacuum cleaner? Edison proudly carried his rather series of failures as his badge of honor. And here we are giving his examples as lessons in our everyday lives. Who knows - one day you might set your own example!

Keep striving towards what you want to achieve. You might fail in your short terms, but keep track of the changes and decisions you make to set that stage right in the way you always wanted.

Get defeated, but don't get lost!

If you know you've done your best up to this point, why would you want to stop doing your best, even though you are disappointed?

If you know you didn't do your best up to this point, it's still up to you to do your best. Maybe you are frustrated and disappointed with yourself for not doing your best. No one can do your best but you.

Do your best one day at a time. Get one day of doing your best, and then get two in a row. Get another in the chain. Mark them on the calendar.

Eventually you will not want to break that chain and doing your best will be a habit. After that, no one will be able to stop you.

Even in the face of your frustration and disappointment, if you just keep doing your best, and only try to control the things you can control, eventually you'll find yourself doing your best every day. If you are doing your best, you will never have to experience failure, regardless of what other people think.

We must fight this at every corner of a loss. This resilience is vital to our future, and even though at the moment we can't feel it or understand it, we must fight through it.

Don't allow the story of today to decide where you will be tomorrow. It's just a story, and it doesn't need to hold any more weight than you allow it to. More importantly, despite the disappointment, we must understand that the story of today does not have to control the story of tomorrow, or even more so, the process of tomorrow.

How you can turn your failures into things that make you soar higher is to ponder why, and how the negative situation happened. Then, ask yourself these questions: "If this and that is what made the negative situation happen, then what can I do to prevent that situation from happening again? What can I do to find the solution to the problem without going at the problem? What can I do to strengthen myself in this area?" Once you have answered those questions in your head, then it is your cue to do those things to help you further reach your goal, climb over those obstacles, or change those obstacles into things that make you soar higher.

How you can get yourself back up is to trace back the things that you've tried and find newer ideas, newer solutions, etc. from the things that lead you to a dead end. A dead end is always a dead end, but a dead end contains many hints and keys to helping you reach where you want to go.

Now back to your goal of changing the world. How would you like to change the world? What is your purpose for changing the world? To be well known? To be famous"? To leave a legend? What are your next steps if you were to achieve your goal? Yes, you can have one goal in mind now, but once you get there what is your next plan? Do you only plan on enjoying the high life of being well known to everyone?

Lastly, success does not come over few failures. Success comes over many failures. And with that, you have the one valuable trait that can help people and change the world's resilience.

Focus on your process and handling defeat with persistence and resilience. The rest will take care of itself.

If you don't taste the pain of failure then you will never able to enjoy the sweetness of success. You must treat failure as a learning or a steeping stone towards success.

In life many times result are not in our favour but attitude towards result which is either positive or negative is always in our hand. Failure should be used as gasoline to fire ourself towards our goals.

A soilder sometime during war lost his life for the protection of the country , So is he failed? . Definitely not. He has done his duty till his last breath without regards of result because he is so much busy in his duty to protect the motherland that he never bother about failure or results. do your work without thinking about results.

Don't think for a second that you're the only person on the planet who failed. Often we look at other's success and assume they have everything together when the reality is that they encounter failure just as much as anyone. Some are better at hiding it than others, but failure is universal. Before you start bashing yourself for not hitting the mark, explore the world of failure and see how vast it truly is.What successful person do you look up to? Take a look at the failures they've encountered in their lives and work. Read biographies, blogs, and listen to speeches. Successful people talk about failure just as much as they talk about success, and it's because they respect how important it is to embrace it. Even the greatest people in our world have fallen, and fallen hard at one point or another. Your friends and family fail too. Think about the failures they have encountered, and remember that you're not alone. It's not to point and laugh, but to show yourself that failure is okay. You're human, just like everybody else.

The only way you will get failure in life is, when you lose hope.Failure is, when you lose your hope and quit the journey. So, chill out and keep going.I will tell one thing, whatever happens in life try to be neutral, stay calm. If you got success don't get so excited because it is also not permanent. If you closely watch people who got success in life, you can see they will stay neutral in their bad and good situations, because they know the failure or success is not going to be with them forever. What you fail at does not define you. You define you. You are capable of achieving great things when you rise above adversity. Let the things you accomplish define you, nothing else. You are making a sincere effort,that matters. You will improve gradually.Good luck, Make yourself proud.

Hopes are alive that's why that saluted spirit is still there,Emboldened attitude is high that's why that little smile is still present there, Stack stops are there but final destination is still awaited, Yes,there is no shortage of struggles in this world but they have to end someday.

It is highly likely that you will identify all important reasons for your failure. Failure always has a set of reasons of which some of them majorly have impacted it. If you would have given up in the middle, you may have missed out few shortcomings on your progress and therefore you may attribute to excuses instead of reasons. On the other hand, if you identify the main reasons for your failure, you greatly improve your chance of winning it elsewhere or it itself again as you overcome irrational fear. There are times when you want to give up, give up on your dreams or give up on yourselves. There are times when people question you or your capabilities. But, believe me there is always that one person who believes in you, who want you to achieve all your dreams, who was with you during your hard times and that person is you;yes you! Even if you have thousand haters, just think about yourself. Never give up, and be confident in what you do. There may be tough times, but the difficulties which you face will make you more determined to achieve your objectives and to win against all the odds.

You must try to remain grounded even when you succeed. Only those shall get success in life, who have no fear of failures and continue to struggle till the end.Neither we nor your parents will be there at every point in life, so learn to stand on your own feet. Follow your passion, never afraid to take risks if it's worth it and work relentlessly towards your goal for sooner or later you will surely achieve it.

Sometimes, you may get anxious if you fail, but always remember that success and failure are the two faces of the same coin and you should always be patient if you fail at any given point of time and try harder to be successful next time.Your Faith and Patience are the biggest tools in helping you achieve the real success. Be in the top 1% and stand out of the crowd and see what happens; You are successful. All the very best!

You have something in you which no one in the world has. Recognise it and work on it.It doesn't matter if you fail;if you keep up with it, someday you are bound to be successful.

Are you so weak to have given up on life just because of some things that went wrong?

Have you come so far in life just to give up now? Is this

what you truly deserve? Can't there be any better outcome of this?

Just know that you have come into this world for a reason. Maybe the most trivial one but yes,there's surely one.There are people out there, who need you,yes.There are thousands of people who need someone
to hear them out. Go to the old age homes, orphanages etc. And speak to them. Look at how strong they are, that in spite of having lost almost everything, they are still fighting to live. To be alive.
Go and help them out. Give them happiness. Become useful to someone. The satisfaction that you'll get after seeing a smile on their face will be priceless.

Giving up is very simple.You have come so far all by yourself. Why give up now? Do you want all those efforts of yours to go waste?

It's ok that no one understands you,because far more important is that you understand yourself and that you know yourself.There are many tough situations in your life and you just can not keep wandering and seeking people's approval who are/will not be significant to you in a matter of time.

I know it is hard to stand alone and it requires huge act of courage and valor.Trust me,you will be fine soon.Everything will be fine soon.

Life gives chances to everybody in one form or other,sometimes early,sometimes late. But yes,it does.Keep faith and keep moving till you get your chance.

The timing isn't always right,but eventually destiny sleeps in.All you need is patience.

This is how the laws of nature work.Since you've seen pain(failure) for a long period of time,now it's time you see a success.Big,so big. That's going to compensate all the loss.

All the pain. All the suffering. All that you need is a positive spirit.

Great things take time. You just need to have patience. Always remember that things which we get very easily don't last long. The same applies to the people around you and you are going to enjoy the long lasting effect on you.

Miracles happen at the most unexpected moments!Think of how it feels,when you make it big leaving everyone awestruck?! Awesome! Isn't it?Wait for the right moment and you're going to get paid for all your efforts.

See,failure is one thing you will have to do before you reach success. Without going through failure you won't get to success. Every successful person had to go through failure and now they have finally made it to success. If you feel as if you will never make it to success then you won't. Those people who failed over and over again and after failing many time they always do one thing and that is never stop. Once you start failing you either have the choice to stay down or you can get up and keep on moving until you make it to your dreams and goals.

Life will never be easy and if it was easy you would have made it to your dreams already but are you there yet?,no right. You have to keep grinding until you make it to success and even once you made it you have to keep on going. Don't feel bad for making mistake's those mistake's should teach you a lesson and that lesson will eventually make you realize what not to do and what to do. Every mistake you have made learn for it don't just let it slide always learn.

Everyday you have to learn something new. Life is about Failing,Learning,Teaching and Achieving. Once you fail you will then learn something new and once you learn you will then teach yourself that something and once you teach yourself that something you will then achieve greater thing's.

Now since you hopefully learn something new what will you do? Will you still be the person that you use to be? or Will you be a new and better person? I am honestly hoping you all learned something from reading this. If you did learn something,so i want to tell you that it's time for all of you to reach for the sky and make it to your dreams. I wish all of you the best of the best.

Just think about it.Find out a reason to live. Do whatever you can do, however small that deed may be, for the people around you. Reach out to anyone who needs help and give them that happiness.

You are much bigger than your problems. Bounce back and overcome the difficulties.The happiness that you will get after doing that will be out of the world.Reach the stars and skies in your chosen career and in your life.

You have to work hard to get what you think. Only those who will risk going too far ,possibly find out how far one can go. You need that one chance to chase your potential because you are irreplacable and once you set your laser focus on what you need and know that the plan and strategy will help then no one can stop you.

Mistakes give you a worthy experience but only if you are willing to learn. Analyze what went wrong and try correcting it. Don't try to reason yourself for the mistake,accept it.

Doing mistake is natural and it is not bad but not learning from mistakes keep you in the same position as you were before.So try, do your best, commit mistakes, acknowledge them, learn from them and bring the best product from within yourself.

We can't go further without making mistakes.So, every chance you take in life love, live and learn from it. Because time is what makes you and breaks you.Mistakes might be distorting but you have to move on and learn not to repeat. And learning is not difficult if you will to do it,just try you will.

Sooner or later or right now you may not be able to give all of you in all you want but that's okay. Wait for the moment, Nothing lasts forever in this wicked world, not even your worries.

Become self -aware and understand the genuine fact that if you can imagine you can create it. Even if the entire world is against you;don't believe it.You can achieve your goal,your purpose of life, A hero is only human, but that's the point. If they can do it, so can you. So, you keep going. You don't give up. You stand tall. You fight. One day,you'll definitely prove them wrong.

Try and try again and again till you succeed,good luck.

CHAPTER SIX

~ A Survivor: Tough Situation,Tough Life. ~

Life is tough. Opportunities will pass you by,just because you are nothing today.People are selfish. It's a tough world. If you ain't already famous,or rich or connected, you will end it rough.

Doors will be shut on you.People Will steal your glory and crash your hopes.You will push and push and yet nothing will happen.Have you ever had a dream? A wonderful dream? But you are too broke to implement it? Too tiny to do it?Too small to accomplish it?

I've been there too many times!People will be saying bad about you every time and then your hopes will be crashed. You will do odd jobs for survival. You will be unable to feed yourself. And yes,you may end up sleeping in the streets.

It happens. Yes,it does but never let them crush your dream.Whatever happens to you,keep dreaming. Even when they crush your hopes,keep dreaming. Even when they turn you away,keep dreaming.Even when they shut you down,keep dreaming.

No one knows what you are capable of except yourself. People will judge you by how you look and by what you have.But please, Fight on! Fight for your place in history. Fight for your glory.Never ever give up.

Even if it means selling all your clothes and sleeping with the dogs,it's okay.But As long as you're still alive,your story is not aver, trust me.

We all fail sometimes in our life.So,does our life stops?Destiny is shaped by our attitude.Right attitude is to go and give our best shot in whatever we do!

What others do in their own life, has mostly no real influence on your own. It is a hard fact to accept, because we have romanticized our thinking by watching movies and reading fiction full of coincidences. Nobody can influence you as much as you yourself can. Stop regretting the chances that didn't come true because somebody didn't do something for you, or the interactions that didn't unfold the way you wanted them to. Move on and be a creator of your own destiny. Be individualistic. Start finding happiness in your own things, start enjoying your own time alone.

If you are on top, you are on top, no matter where the others are. If someone's success and failure doesn't make any difference to you, you are at peace. In fact, if you learn to celebrate someone else's success it will make you happier.

See,we will always face problems in our life.The most important part of our problems is how we choose to deal with them.You will not always be able to fix everything and that is okay.One thing i want to tell you that,a problem is only a problem if you see it but if you look for the solution then there isn't a problem.

Your present is the only thing you have in control, regretting about the past and worrying about the future is not going to solve any problem for youIf you want to be a better person, you need to stop dwelling on the past and worrying about the future.

It's easy to go along with what everyone else is doing because humans instinctively want to be part of a herd.Fighting that, in a way, is fighting human nature.But it just takes a little bit of observation to realize that the crowd is not always a good place to be.Being different from the crowd leads to bigger and better things.If you want to improve your life in any way, observe what everyone else is doing and do the opposite.We are all gifted with energy to find a success in our life, but fail to gather a courage which is required to reach heights of success and end up clinging to the things that are familiar to us.We need to free ourselves from our comfort zone to explore new opportunities and find a success beyond our capacity.

Create a positive atmosphere - Positivity, happiness, excitement and joy are all things you can have and create as long as you practice them. You get more done when you are happy, are less likely to feel attacked when happy and are kinder, nicer and overall a better person.

Own up to your mistakes - Everyone makes them and a lot of people made worse mistakes than you have. Own up to your own mistakes and solve the problems you created. This is your life, meaning it is yourresponsibility, for better or for worse.

Listen to the people around you - It's not about you. Every person has their own life to live and is the main character of another story! Sit down and watch their story unfold. Become interested in them instead of

When we experience hard times(problems), these phases break us from inside more than we could think.
Overcoming it has mostly three possibilities: Learning to live with it, defeating it, or accepting defeat;in this possibilities we learn different things i.e patience through

learning to live with it, ability to fight by not allowing your self to get weak ,and the third one, even though looks like failure has the most impact, it

tells us our limitations, strengths, weakness, patience, and most of all it makes us understand that always in

life we don't succeed and side times might fail, but we shouldn't give up and have hope that time will heal all wound.

We want our dreams to be true. We want our parents to be proud of us, our success and everything we do. So you should know for what you are doing, and how you will contribute your knowledge to society and to our country. So ;decide what you want to do and start moving towards it without any fear and most important whatever the thing you want to do, do that thing only otherwise no success.

We never try to find solutions in happy conditions because we are at peace. Solutions to the problem, gives us experience and we become stronger when we know how to deal with the situation.

So moral of the story is, your existence is never influenced by someone else. What's meant for you will always find its way. And if you want to change it, you always can. It's not easy. Not everyone's got a stomach for it. It takes a lot of time, but it can happen.

Sometimes life can be rough and we need some help to push through. Please use these to help you, and I hope you can stay positive through your days.

Calm yourselt and tell yourself that;if everyone is probably whiling away time right now, let me stand out from this ludicrous crowd. Let me try to make a difference, not for anyone else, just me.

Believe in own capabilities, and think about those who have done already great work in the same area, in which area you want to do something. If they can do, then why can't you be the next one of them. Who are great and unique achiever, they are not out of this planet, they are from the same planet,you just need to recognize your potential and capabilities.

Everything that glitters is not gold. A decision is not a text that whenever we want. we can replace it with a new one. Every decision leaves an indelible impression on our life. It changes the course of our life. It makes us happy or sad. But how could one predict the outcome of one's decision? I think it is destiny and not the decision which gets one success.

It has to come from within you; you have to ask yourself how badly you want it, and how much are you willing to sacrifice for it. Keep your dreams alive. Understand to achieve anything requires faith and belief in yourself, vision, hard work, determination, and dedication. Remember all things are possible for those who believe. It is just a matter of hard work.

You are essentially who you create yourself to be and all that occurs in your life is the result of your own making. The true measure of success is how many times you can bounce back from failure and that is motivation.Someone has truly said,Only you can change my life;no one can do it for me.

Each and every one of us has those days when we are just not relaxed; we are mentally and physically drained. — When this happens, it's time to motivate ourselves and overcome the hurdles in our life. We should keep it in mind that most of the important things in the world have been accomplished by people who have motivated themselves and kept on trying when there seemed to be no hope at all.

The ultimate measure of a man is not where he stands in moments of comfort and convenience but where times of challenge and controversy. There are many rewards and punishments in life. If you are smart then you will try to optimize your rewards and minimize the punishments with a realistic appraisal of your abilities so that you don't crash and burn trying to do the impossible or desiring what you can't have.

Learn to celebrate yourself, when nobody else celebrates you. It's not up to other people motivation? to keep you encouraged. It's up to you to keep yourself motivated and happy. Encouragement and motivation should come from the within.

When you are yourself you show who you really are. People like people who are genuine. When you are being genuine, you find friends that value you for who you are. When you act out to be someone you are not, you put up a facade to the true genuine " you" that only builds walls between you and other people. Unless you like the guessing game of who you are today, putting up masks do not contribute to your whole personality. People who are genuine show their vulnerabilities, their true self and being open is the best thing to be because that is who you are truly. When you are true to yourself, you don't even have to lie, make up a story or be someone else because people will value the real you.

You don't need to be the fastest.You don't need to be the wisest.You don't need to be the smartest.You don't need to be the most brilliant.All you need is courage.All you need is the will to try. All you need is the faith to believe it is possible.All you need is to believe in yourself, that you can do it.

There can never be another you - a pirate copy or a perfect copy of you.

There is not a single person in the whole wide world like you.

Nobody shares the same space, time, energy and resources.

No one can think, speak and act like you.

The greatest scientist in the world cannot develop anything that is remotely similar to you.

The best computer cannot perform like your brain and your bodily systems.

The latest advancement in medical and life sciences cannot replicate the intricate workings in your body, mind and spirit.

The wisest persons cannot explain to you about yourself.

They cannot understand what made you the person that you are and the genius that dwells within your being.

You are one of the greatest blessings that has happened and will ever happen in your life.

You are created with almost unlimited potential and infinite amount of possibilities.

You are gifted with a unique personality, capacity and set of abilities.

You have a vast reservoir of energy that can be used to make a positive difference to people and the environment.

Nothing should ever make you think otherwise and cause you to love less of yourself.

Nobody should stop you from living a life of love and loving the best of life.

No one throughout the passage of time has suffered the same pain or enjoyed the same pleasure as you.

You and you alone have gone through unique moments, experiences and achievements.

Keep up the Fight. Keep your dreams and hope alive.Failure is not the end,it's the beginning of a legacy!

Be grateful. Remember,you are one in a countless ones that could've existed. Just for the life you got, the things you have, the calamities you're spared from. Not everyone has this easy with life and you know you're way much better than most people out there.

CHAPTER SEVEN

~ Don't lose hope: Be someone you would be proud to know. ~

We listen more to what others say instead of listening to ourselves. Ignore what others say. You must have heard the popular Hindi saying-'Kuch to log kahenge,logon ka kam hai kehna'.

We forget that our dreams are more important to us than others.We forget that it depends on us how we fulfill our dreams and not the judgement of other people.

So, when you are surrounded by people who constantly demoralize you just keep quiet and work constantly towards your goal. You don't need to defend yourself by arguing with them. Prove yourself through your actions.Take it as a challenge. You shouldn't be aiming at proving yourself to those people. You should aim at completing your dream to prove that fact that you had it in you!

I know,its tough to work in an environment full of negativity, but never let that negativity contaminate your ideas and mindset.You should completely focus on you goals and not what others say. It's a difficult job but not impossible. Afterall,they would never know how much your dreams mean to you! People are meant to demotivate you. They do this because they themselves are demotivated. Yes, they makes us frustrated. They want to see you suffer. So now my question is do you want to get suffered because of others? Stop thinking of others .Just be yourself, no need to prove them.

The problem is inside you and the solution also lies beneath.The fruits of hardwork are never lost. They are going to show up very soon. Don't lose hope. Just stay patient and watch the drama that's going to unfold in stages.

This is no time to sit and get dejected. You are going to be excited about it. This is nothing new. No bad luck is running in your fate. And no star is responsible for this, all that you need is a positive spirit.Great things take time. You just need to have patience. Always remember that things which we get very easily don't last long.The same applies to the people around you and you are going to enjoy the long lasting effect on you.

You should enjoy every moment while you are studying.Believe me,the journey is more pleasing and satisfying than the destination.Miracles happen at the most unexpected moments. You're about to relish the feeling! Think of how it feels,when you make it big leaving everyone awestruck?Now go back to work and keep doing it. Wait for the right moment and you're going to get paid for all your hard work and efforts.

You are priceless, let your emotions rule the world. There are many things in this world to do, focus on your career, your goals, your dreams. Stay away from negativity, stay away. There are many people who are worried about their future, my friend, everything will be alright. You are here for a reason. Look up, don't feel sad. Big things are waiting for you, you and your mind need relaxation. Go on a long weekend, watch motivational videos, talk to good people.

Block all unnecessary people from your life. Life is big, bigger than we all think, we are small puppets over here, we don't even know where we will be in the next few years. I never thought of writing documents/blogs and all. Forget everything, start something new. Tomorrow when you wake up, promise yourself that you will shine, you will do something big. Be that rare person whom everyone respects.

Be yourself and if you still need some motivation, go and slap yourself in front of the mirror and ask
yourself, about your mistakes. Promise me that you will win? Don't run from anything, just win. Be a winner. Will you? Life is so worthwhile, and no matter what has happened to you, no matter what you're background is, no matter what your past is, each of us deserve to be happy. Bad things happen, but that doesn't mean that they need to define our life.

We have things that happen to us, and yes, they shape us, they mould us. Because in the end what defines you is how you react, are the decisions that you make. So, I hope that whether you're faced with, whatever you deal with, you just remember that you are who you decide to be. You are captain of your destiny. You are the one that decides who you are.

Just never give up and never stop believing in yourself. Stop thinking about how people judge you. Nobody has the right to judge you except your parents. Even if you fail,it doesn't mean those others were right about you being incapable of achieving your goals.It means you need to try once again with a different approach.If you don't believe in yourself nobody will believe in you.

From time to time you'll have instances when things will not go your way. But do not give up just because the road is difficult. You will fall down but you will get up again and that's what determines you not your failures.Sometimes you'll be in a situation where you can't decide where to go. What if, if you choose the first path and failed. Here come's the role of failure in life. Next time when you're facing the same situation then you know that which track to choose.

Some times you need to think like the way other's think and need to accept the reality that every thing can't go the way they wish then no one would suffer so, everyone come through a phase where they feel low and depressed and this in a part of life. Life is only when you face difficulties not when every thing goes in a cool manner.God tests eveyone and we need to face our problems and learn how to solve it by our own way. We may get some help but know that you need to run in the race if you need to win not let other run behalf of you. Every thing has a reason only if you stop expecting things like really these things you will come out of depression.

Stop running behind what is not there with you be happy with what is with you and learn to value it, who knows you will get what you desire. Be happy and thankful for what you've got and never run behind anything like mad so that when you lose you don't lose yourself. Life is a short journey with many experiences so just let it go with the flow.

- Stop Judging:

Spend your time in knowing yourself rather than wasting it by judging others. You never know what they're going through (may be good or bad), judging them won't affect you at first but it will surely instigate a feeling of negativity within you.

- Stop Comparing:

This is one of the worst things one can do to oneself. Usually, we do compare ourselves with someone who is better than us, which in turn makes us feel sad. It would be better if we start comparing us to ourselves and become a better individual.

- Stop Assuming:

Generally, we assume things and start behaving as per our assumptions. Never ever do this. If you feel something, better clear it at the very first moment rather than assuming it.

- Stop Regretting:

You'll find people around your corner those first do things and then regret it later. I mean why? They forget that it was the first thing that they wanted to do at the first moment and still regret. We should overcome this feeling of regret and accept that this is what we wanted.

I have been seeing the world with the cruelness.Everyone has it's own attitude and thinking of there own profit. I feel very bad for the poor people, whenever I saw them begging for live, some is selling fruits or vegetables in the summer's sunlight that no one wants to buy. Why these things aren't getting government attention?

I pray to God everyday, bless me that I could do something for them.Another thing I want to change is,No one should be rich and no one should be poor in this world.Everyone should have wealth regarding their needs to live. But, unfortunately no such thing is in my hands to change. I know it's not easy but I am going to do it anyway. I dream to make my life count.

I dream to die as a content person who had no regrets. I want to die as a person who followed her dreams. As a person who faced many failures but she never gave up and kept doing what she wished to do. Our dreams are not just a dream, they are the reasons why we try to wake up every morning despite having depression. Our dreams are the reason why we all are willing to overcome depression.

Best of luck and lots of good wishes.

Finally want to say,If you win;you might be known to the world.If you lose,you know the world what it is.

CHAPTER EIGHT

~ Smile: The mantra to a successful life. ~

The most important thing in life is to realise the fact that it is short and you only have one shot, so make the best of it.

We sometimes complicate our lives with too many worries about unclear matters that we think might pop up in the future.But that is never going to help us move forward, it'll only drain the happiness from our daily lives.

Life is too short to over complicate it with unwanted worries, hatred, jealousy.

In this unreal world, with whomever we all meet asks do you have a career? Do you own a house as if life was some kind of grocery list but no one asks us are we happy? Think for a second! Did anyone?

A rare case as usual in this unreal world.

Trust me, if one makes this the tenet of living, life will become a lot more bright and better. Life is no smooth sailing, we all have our own set of experiences (both good and bad), trials and lessons which make us what we are!

People around us are all playing supporting roles in our life, and eventually everyone around us will drift away with time.

Nowadays,truth is that we are much busy in our complicated lives and busy schedule.Students; they are busy in getting good grades as they have pressure from family or they want to prove their fellow mates that I am the best one. ,due to that slot of students are suffering from Anxiety ,stress,depression like problems,the age where they are so innocent to learn something has heroine the age of just grasping the things ,instead of enjoying the things ,and instead of doing the things with fun,is being done under pressure of families.Yes, I totally agree that in this competitive environment it is difficult to survive.

If you don't have degrees but of what use is this your life,if you can't lead it in a simple way,happiest way.So ,i must say them to keep peace with their lives and do the things that gives you happiness,not do the things under pressure just do the things you like to dojust explore yourself because in this circumstances you are losing your own identity and trying to become what others want,So guys explore yourself. Don't run behind the things that you are not made of.Figure out your interests but that will give inner happiness and satisfaction.

We are all behind money. No more a simple lifestyle. Its just money money money with growing ego. If you have money, you are respected. Like how we in today's world, we have big house but a small family. Similarly it is more humans and less humanity.

With whomever we all meet asks do you have a career? Do you own a house as if life was some kind of grocery list but no one asks us are we happy? Think for a second! Did anyone? A rare case as usual in this unreal world. Trust me, if one makes this the tenet of living, life will become a lot more bright and better.

Life is no smooth sailing, we all have our own set of experiences (both good and bad), trials and lessons which make us what we are! People around us are all playing supporting roles in our life, and eventually everyone around us will drift away with time.

We should always remain happy and keep a smile on our face whatever be the situation because our inner happiness matters the most and that's the most important thing in life. It's important that you understand the value of life.

Find people who are kind and genuinely care about you, whose company you enjoy. These are not very easy to find, so make sure you hang on to the ones you do meet. This should be the #1 priority in your life. Don't put your career ahead of it, except for short periods of time. Unless you're a sociopath, nothing else has as great a potential to contribute to your happiness as positive interactions with other people.

Find something you really enjoy doing. Even if you can't make a career out of it, make it a priority in your life. Go rock climbing. Build a ship in a bottle. Design a website. Human beings have an innate need to be challenged and to improve themselves. You will derive great satisfaction from your achievements and personal growth.

Avoid feeling threatened by people who are better than you. Even if you can never be as good as them at something, so what? Don't judge other people. It won't do them any good, and it'll make you unhappy, too. Live and let live.

A human being is as big as his dreams. And the bridge between dream and reality is work. So, you have got to work hard, really hard. There is no one to drive you, you have to drive yourself, be the driver!

You have to grow your ethical values in order to form your dreams into reality. Values determine what is right and what is wrong, and doing what is right or wrong is what is meant by ethics. The situation you are in, regardless of bad or good, you are responsible for it. If you are not capable of taking control of your present which can be in your hand, by taking a careful and cautious step in every moment of your life, then how can you think about the future! The steps you take now, it will become the past and it will make a more solid base for your present and also for your very next future. If you are a young entrepreneur or businessperson, you must hold the ability to make ethical decisions. With a view to making ethical decisions, it is essential and wise to perceive and eliminate unethical options and select the best ethical alternative.

You have to be honest and direct with yourself and others. How would you feel if a loved one or business partner lied to you? Chances are you would see that as a violation of your trust. If you want to develop your ethics as a youth and a better person in either your personal or your professional life, you should always tell the truth and state as clearly as possible what you are trying to convey. Do you want to help the people you are surrounded in different conditions of your life or not? Being helpful is one of the easiest and most effective ways to motivate yourself. The more you help others, the better you are going to feel about yourself and everyone around you.

Do not let frustration wash over you. Rather, let those most positive memories, the memories of your biggest successes, wash over you, boosting your motivation.

Replace unhealthy routines with healthy ones, and interlace them with variety. It keeps you alert, and checks boredom and routine fatigue.

Every day, learn something new. Do something for the first time. It keeps you sharp. And over time you'll know a little about so much, which will make you more interesting and relevant.

Take risks. Experiment. Learn and grow and evolve. Improve yourself with every opportunity. Commit to working on you, and becoming good at something that interests you.

The secret of happiness is always with you but you don't realize it until some intruder comes and messes your life. So,never go in search of happiness as.it is always with in you.

A bitter truth is that;your will is insufficient to manage the task. Once your expectations are not met you will feel unsatisfied. Obviously, having no expectations is the key to keeping yourself happy with what life offers you every day. Happiness is simply a decision. Status is what motives people to work themselves to death to get others to acknowledge them as worthy to be part of their tribe. People desperately want others to miss them if they are not around anymore. If you want to be content in life just do not care what other people think by making God the one you are accountable to. If you are true to that, others may see your truth or not. Most will not see. I never care what others think because they know nothing about me or God. It can be a lonely untrod path, but it is yours.

You can never know true happiness if you keep chasing wealth, power and prestige with the hope to enjoy happiness in future.

Redefine happiness. We create our schematic of what happiness means in our own minds. That's why what makes one person happy, may not make another person happy at all. We don't realize how much control we really have over this 'happiness' mechanic. We first decide what we think happiness is, then we wait for that to happen to give ourselves permission to be happy.That is absolutely how the mind works. It's not a 'path', or a belief, it is the cognitive mechanic.

We control the valve. Does making the bed make you happy? If not, why not? Are you not happy to have it done? If so, you actually can teach yourself to be happy making the bed. You like the results. Doing is achieving those results. What's the difference then between making the bed and enjoying the results when its all a part of happiness? We make ourselves unhappy by how limited we allow happiness to be. In truth, happiness is a gift you give to the world, not the other way around.

We become more happy by retraining the mind, to redefine, to be open to new thought processes and be willing to change.

Odd thing about life is that there are always a lot smarter, more capable, and better talented people that could easily do what you find yourself doing in your life. Just remember that despite those facts they are not doing what you found important to do because they found different challenges more important to them to spend their time on. That makes you irreplaceable.

It's important that you make each day worth. It's important to be happy everyday. Enjoy the little things in life, because one day you will look back, and realize those where the big things. So, what is most important is that no matter how harsh or cruel the present times maybe, we continue to push ourselves to move forward.

Nothing is going to last forever, not even your sadness. Remember that. Just because your life has seen a dark phase, you shouldn't miss the beauty of a coming sunrise.

If you fall down 7 times, get up 8 times: Be your own hero, pick yourself when you have to,but make sure you complete the journey. And when you carry ever lasting hope, the journey will become better.

Set some principles of life that you think or that which really matters to you and stick by them no matter what. I promise you that you'll have tough times, even worst times but then comes the best time of your life.

1.Try to forgive more often, everybody makes mistakes, remember that even you do.

2.Only make promises that you are sure to follow through.

3.Tell the truth, no matter what, tell it.

4.Be more grateful. Value the people in your life, no matter how small a role they play, be thankful and respectful.

5.Always believe in yourself, think good, think positive.

6.Never compare yourself with others.

7.Remember that, if everythings not well then its not the end, don't give up.

8.Also remember that you can achieve anything you want if you will yourself to it.

9.Remember whatever you face in life are the effects of your actions anyways;if you are being good then you will be taken to good some way or the other.

10.Don't copy others path rather create your own destiny, yes you can learn a lot from others life but that doesn't mean you will have the same life instead learn from others and make wise decisions in your life and live your passion.

11.Above all, always keep smiling and don't forget to enjoy the little things in life.

There is no reason for you to be sad, you are alive and you can do something about the problem.Atleast you are alive. Pleasure and happiness are two different things. So never take stupid decisions . Live in present, not in future. There are people out there who are very rich but not happy. Yes you must find comfort, need through money,it makes sense but not happiness. You need to understand this concept.

You are unique, you don't need to become like any other. You are what you are. It is what it is !

When you really feel like quitting something good, just look back and remind yourself of the long way you have traveled. Just save yourself from this weak moment. You will go a long way if you can survive this difficult moment. This is what is important in life.

Live the best life, good luck!

CHAPTER NINE

~ No struggle,no progress: The world is yet to be discovered. ~`

BELIEVE IN OURSELF :The most important thing before achieving success is to believe in it. At every single moment of your day, your success and dream should be in your mind.You cannot achieve
success until you have imagined it how it looks. You need to invest some time of your day
in dreaming about your success.

The things that you will get after succeeding, how your life will be.You should be able to
feel the moment of your success every single moment. You should wake with it, eat with
it, sleep with it and drink with it. Every single day a lot of times you might face the hard
reality, and you will feel it's not possible to achieve it, it is so difficult to achieve it but
irrespective of these facts you have to believe in it.

Your success should be crystal clear in your heart. As told in our Ramayana Hanuman
was having Lord Ram in his heart and when he let people

see across his heart there was a
picture of his Lord. Your success should be such clear.

DON'T GIVE UP :For instance, when we buy things from online we try a lot of stuff and then decide what to buy. Similarly, in order to achieve success, you have to try things without trying you cannot succeed.

If giving up would be an option then Virat Kohli could never become the best cricketer. Lionel Messi could never become the best footballer. Michael Jordon could never be the best basketball player. Elon Musk, Thomas Edison, Jrd Tata, Sandeep Maheshwari,these people should never become so great as they are today.So don't give up and work hard till you achieve your goals and success.

SMALL ACT,BIG DIFFERENCE :Usain bolt is the fastest man on Earth, we all know that but did he started running so fast from the day he was b5orn. The answer is no. Like any other kid, he also started by crawling. He first learned to crawl, then started walking and then learned the art of running and with the time he becomes the fastest person on Earth.He might have fallen thousands of times before he learns to walk but he never gave up.

The most important thing towards any goal is taking your first step. If you stuck yourself thinking that what to do after my first step, you will never be able to take it. And believe me, you just need to take
your first step rest will be arranged in accordance automatically.

Because the luck also favors the bravest. If you are brave enough to take your first step then no doubt you will easily achieve your destination easily.

Most of the successful people when started their companies, started with something else and now doing a completely different thing today but they were brave enough to start thus they were blessed with the gift of success.

Do you remember the lesson from your physics notebook? The topic of "Moment of Inertia". It taught us that when an object is standing it takes a lot of force to start it and once it is started it is easy to carry it forward. The same is true of your destiny. Just make yourself courageous to take the first step.

BE POSITIVE : The positive thoughts have a great impact on our lives. You are what you think about
yourself. What we think in our daily life about yourself and our life, our subconscious mind will make it true in reality. Thus it is always said to think positive because we will become what we will think and things will also work in accordance with it.

Acting positively is always important because we have a long list of people who were succeeded after a long failure in their life but they were succeeded later. It was possible just because they were positive about the things they were doing. They had a firm belief in their ideas and themselves that made them great.

Thomas Edison failed 1o,000 times but every time he failed he had a clear vision that he was going right and he was positive enough to achieve success and he becomes successful in his 10,001 th attempt. So you need to have a lot of faith patience, belief and yes you have to act positively.

See,If you go crazy for your dream to be true. It's all about your own hardwork,consistency and the firm self believe system on yourself.If you want your dream ;it's your own choice and all the way its in your own hand.Work for it ,give your best,and just be positive; keep no doubt on your capability,you'll definitely get your dream true.

We have all seen rich people die unhappy. Money brings happiness, temporarily. We should all strive to do better, achieve our goals, earn more, be able to enjoy material things in life. But we should recognize that while its good to have these things, they do not bring long term happiness. In 20 years, we will look back on the technologies we have today and wonder what the fuss is about. It will look very antiquated, just like the cassette player. My point is that all these material things only bring temporary happiness. I am very glad to be able to enjoy these material goods but I know I can't bring them with me when I die and they only bring joy that will eventually dissipate. So while I enjoy them, I make sure I do not attach too much importance to them.

We all unconsciously desire the respect and admiration of others. It strokes our egos and we feel hurt when we don't get the friendship or attention from others.What you think of yourself is important.You have to be your own best friend.Don't let anyone tell you its conceited to think this way.

Do not envy others or let allow jealousy to seize your mind. This is very important as being humans we are naturally envious and jealous of people we perceive to be better. Be always guarded against these two feelings as they can really ruin your life and make you very unhappy. But how does one prevent these thoughts from overwhelming them? Simple. It goes back to the realization that life is short and that materialism is not that important.

Sometimes people come into your life and it becomes obvious that they were meant to be part of your life, they were meant to serve some kind of purpose in your life, not necessarily positive, maybe to teach you lessons and sometimes help you figure out who you are or whom you are supposed to be.

You are never certain about who these people may be, roommate, neighbours, lecturers, friends, lovers, parent, brothers, sisters, inlaws, sometimes they are complete strangers, but when you take an introspective analysis of your experience with them, you will see that they played a part in whom you are today or who you are becoming.

Sometimes things happen to you that may seem horrible, painful, and unfair at first, I'm speaking from personal experience, but as you reflect on things you discover that without overcoming those obstacles you would have never realized your potential, strength, willpower, or know your true self.

Illness, injury, heart breaks, flop on moments of greatness, and sheer stupidity all occur to test the limits of our soul and readiness for the next stage in our earthly pilgrimage.

Without these tests, whatever they may be, life would be like a smoothly paved straight flat road to nowhere. It would be safe and comfortable, but dull and utterly pointless.

The people we meet on our journey through life are the people who affect and effect our life, and the success and downfalls we experience, are suppose to help create who we are and whom we will become.

Even the bad experiences can be learned from. In fact, sometimes they are proponent shaper of our destiny.

If someone loves you, give love back to them in whatever way you can, not only because they love you, but because in a way, they are teaching you to love and how to open your heart and eyes to the world.

If someone hurts you, betrays you, breaks your heart, forgive them for with what you feel you will learn to guild your heart, mind and actions with diligence and to be cautious of how and whom you open your conciouseness to.

Make every day count. Appreciate every moment and take from those moments everything that you can possibly take, you will never experience those moment again, those moment are like classroom on your path through life. Talk to people that you have never talked to before, and listen to what they have to say.

Let yourself fall in love, break free, and set your sights high. Hold your head up because you have every right to do so, you are an incredible being.

Stand in the mirror and tell yourself you are a great person and believe in yourself, for if you don't believe in yourself, it will be difficult for others to believe in you.

You have unlimited potentials, you can make life anything you wish, but make it the things that inspire peace, love and kindness. Create your own life and then go out and live it with absolutely no regrets.

Take everyday serious, learn a lesson in life each day that you live.

Today is the tomorrow you were talking about yesterday, and here it is almost gone, it's going to be called yesterday in the next few hours, make everyday count even though it is 1% better.

The more efforts you put towards your goals, the better would be the end-results.The distancebetween dreams and reality is called action.Thinking about something isn't enough, you do need to work hard for it. Next, you need to believe that what you dreamt of will come true.

Have patience. At times, things take longer than expected. Good things come to you whenyou least expect them and when the time is perfect for them to happen. So, dream until your dreamcomes true.

If you believe in something that you wish to achieve, if you know that you have the capacity to go out and face the storms, beat all the odds and get back on your feet every time you fall, then no matter what others say to you, you will succeed.People will come and doubt you, but if you are patient enough and keep your efforts in the right direction, fate will take its course. Afterall,All good things to those who wait.

CHAPTER TEN

~ Miracles happen: The purpose of life. ~

Life do have a purpose! And what's that?The answer is that we are in this universe to explore it and extract the most out of it.

Life is all about what you think of it. How you live your life defines your perspective towards life. Life could be simple or purposeful. Either you will die one day without knowing why you come to this world and what you did in your whole life or you find a purpose of life.

Some people just born, eat, grow, and die that's what every other species of world do. Some people born, find some purpose of life, work for that purpose and accomplishes that and then when they die they are very much satisfied with their life.They have a deep happiness inside that their life were meaningful. They leave their effect to this life.

Firstly,I don't think we should waste our time thinking on such question,a simple logical argument for people who say (and if you are one them,for you) that 'It is a waste of time and stop asking this question and live your life.' is - Imagine when you'll be old, on a bed, counting your last few breaths, just about to close your eyes, what will it be going through your mind;that you never did anything worthwhile, you never made someone cry tears of joy, you haven't done anything for which people will remember you (and not in their memory or as a character in a textbook) and just lived away your life thinking about your personal happiness.

However, just make sure that you don't overthink and spend your time on thinking rather than actually living. You have not lived until you have done something for someone who can never repay you.

So, think of it now, have you ever done something like this? If you see a person driving a Porsche, wearing a gold plated Rolex watch, please don't think that he has lived a lot better life, and is a lot more successful than you, because its a possibility that even he hasn't lived yet.

If you don't know the purpose of your life, for now make this as your purpose - Live everyday;and you know what i mean by live - do something for someone who can never repay you.And while doing that you'll finally find your purpose.

Goals are what you want to get from your life. It can be name, fame, money, health, etc.You can't change your life if you have no goals. No change in life means you could not fulfill your wishes.Next 20 years you will be in the same condition , where you are now. It will be worse than now.You can't achieve even a single thing in life, which you will regret later.You can't experience amazing feelings, when you get what you want after achieving your goals. You will spend your life as Mediocre. In the end of your life you will have many regrets.If you have a goal you are clear of what you you are doing, why you are doing and at the end what result you can get,life will become without goals. You will live each day but you will not be advancing. You will not have any direction in your life.

It is always up to you, and which will satisfy you in the end and get that feeling where you can say I am happy I was born to do this, I was born to create a difference in the time line in which one is living.

One should have goal in their own life so that once when you are dead or while when you have a few moments left in your life and you are going to die, you should have zero regrets and should get you in thinking that was the purpose in your life.

You can't get a perfect shot until you have a target and a good aim.So have a goal, plan to achieve that goal and actually achieve it.

If you focus on your dream and keep doing work on it, you shall definitely win. Just remember success isn't easy, its too easy. Keep doing work, follow your passion. Don't kill time. If you loose the first time, don't worry. You'll win the second time.

What is the meaning of your existence in this universe? All achievements start with a burning desire:When you will be a failure , no body cares,when you will become successful very few will truely care. Don't be in a hurry, things take time.

Initially you will even find it difficult to start, but don't lose hope. You aren't a bad person. You are making mistakes. Everyone makes mistakes, and everyone can reduce their mistakes; that's okay, just try again and again. Ignore what other people are doing. You are doing this for yourself, in a way that works for you, because you deserve success. Let them be annoyed, or make fun, or whatever.Keep going. Push yourself, only then you can move forward.

Everyone has a unique purpose of existence, since everyone among the 7 billion of us is a unique personality, "There are 7 billion different ways to live." Do remember this: Don't waste your time living someone else's life.

Every individual is trying to change his or herself,but the fun that lies in changing the world is completely different.There is no fun in walking without falling, the fun that lies in recovering after falling again and again is completely different.

Never give up because if you give up now, you'll never come to know what you are capable of.It means that - There may be tough times, but the difficulties which you face will make you more determined to achieve your objectives and to win against all the odds. Chase your dreams and never give up even when you fail.Act as if nothing happened.Try again and again.

A day would arrive, success would embrace you in her arms. There are times when you want to give up, give up on your dreams or give up on yourselves.There are times when people question you or your capabilities.There are times when people leave you when you need them the most.But, believe me there is always that one person who believes in you, who cares for you, who want you to achieve all your dreams, who was with you during your hard times and that person is you,yes you.Even if you have 1000 haters, just think there is still that one person.Never give up atleast for the sake of yourself.

Before you give up think about why you held on so long. If you still give up, it only means that you never wanted it. Remember that success in life comes when you simply refuse to give up, with goals so strong that obstacles, failure and loss only act as motivation. Never stop trying, never stop believing, never give up, your day will come.Remember, the harder the struggle, the more glorious the triumph. Therefore, stay strong, stay positive and never even think of giving up.

Just before you are about to give up in life, remember the efforts you have put in so far to get there.Remember the efforts and the time that will be wasted if you chose to not go further. It will be then you will gather courage to make the best choice for yourself in life. Most people fail to achieve their true potential in their life because they give up too qukidy. You have to read the biographies of great men to reali7e that they succeeded in life only after extraordinary large failures. Michael Jordan, the legendary American professional basketball player said, I have missed more than 9,000 shots in my career. I have lost almost 300 games. On 26 occasions I have been entrusted to take the game winning shot, and I missed. I have failed over and over and over again in my life. And that is why I succeed. Thomas A. Edison too failed loom) times before he invented the bulb. He, however, did not do the same thing for 10,000 times as he said, I have not failed.

I've just found 10,000 ways that won't work.Had Edison tried to do the same thing for even one million times, he would have never succeeded. You must give up those things where you are unlikely to succeed to focus on those things where you can succeed.If you keep doing the same thing forever without applying your mind about your ability to succeed in the mission, you are sure loser.It is so because you are losing the opportunity of winning in those fields where you have the ability to succeed.If you quit you will never get what you want, but if you keep trying you will find a way to get what you want. When you never give up and fight for something, be all positive.

Work towards the goal with an attitude of "I am going succeed, its me who's going to win". Don't be with an attitude "I will try my best". Don't use the word try. Tell yourself you are going to win this thing. There is no other way to go. Don't give yourself another choice. Go all in. Do whatever it takes. Keep telling yourself that you are going to win this thing.And one day, you will. Keep going on until that day comes!

Good things come to those who believe, better things come to those who are patient and the best things come to those who don't give up

If you are focused towards your goal, if you are persistent then no one can stop you from achieving your goal.If you are aiming towards anything higher then you should be capable enough to sacrifice something,because success in life is directly proportional to sacrifices you make. And these sacrifices should not be supported by a feeling of remorse but by a feeling of pride and dilligency.Keep yourself busy, don't let negative thoughts conquer your mind, don't worry about the outcomes rather focus on your preparation, outcome will surely be in your favour.

I feel like writing a lot more but its already gone too long.This is so less to say, there's still a lot to say about life. Each step in life makes you learn a new lesson, nobody is a loser in this life game, if the one is thinking himself as a loser.

9 798885 691949

Printed by Libri Plureos GmbH in Hamburg,
Germany